CRIMCOMICS

BIOLOGY AND CRIMINALITY

KRISTA S. GEHRING

WRITER

MICHAEL R. BATISTA

ARTIST

PATRICK M. POLLARD

INKER

CHERYL L. WALLACE

LETTERER

New York   Oxford

OXFORD UNIVERSITY PRESS

Dedication
To Nicky Rafter,
You helped create this issue more than you will ever know.

—KRISTA S. GEHRING

To Br. Frederick Eid,
You taught me the importance of reference, and happy accidents.

—MICHAEL R. BATISTA

FOREWORD

"A picture is worth a thousand words." This old saying is the first thing that came to my mind upon reviewing Krista Gehring and Michael Batista's innovative *CrimComics*. This is an important work because after almost a century of the dominance of sociology in criminology, which essentially meant that criminology concerned itself exclusively with environmental explanations of criminal behavior, criminology is moving toward a biosocial perspective. All sciences move forward if they are indeed sciences, but until recently, while the natural sciences (genetics, neuroscience, etc.) were moving ahead at warp speed, criminology did so at a snail's pace. In the early 1980s, a few (very few) criminologists realized that the natural sciences have a bounty of gifts for them just waiting to be accepted. What moves any science forward is the invention of new technology, not new theories. Just as the telescope and the microscope opened up new worlds of possibility for the physicist and the biologist, the ability to easily obtain DNA profiles and information about a person's brain via a variety of scanning techniques will prove immensely useful to criminologists. *CrimComics* explains these rather complicated techniques, and the theories to which they are applied, to students in simple *and visual* fashion.

Because of these technologies, the field of criminology is now undergoing a paradigm shift toward a biosocial approach. A growing number of criminologists are either being converted to the approach by the evidence, or are being turned out with their PhDs by brilliant scholars such as John Wright at the University of Cincinnati and Kevin Beaver at Florida State University, and by former students of these giants at universities across the country. Beaver was a student of Wright; Wright was a student of Francis Cullen, who is a current "big name" champion of the biosocial perspective. Dr. Cullen was a student of such sociological luminaries as Thomas Merton and Richard Cloward; thus Dr. Cullen personifies the merging of the sociological and the biological.

A skeptic may pour scorn on the notion of learning anything from a book laid out like a childhood comic book. These folks would be fooling themselves. In the "bad old days," when PhD students had to pass translation exams in two foreign languages, as well as pass classes, endure two weeks of comprehensive exams, and write a dissertation, my biggest fear was the language requirement because aside from knowing a little German, I did not take a language in high school. My two elected languages were German and French. I lived in Michigan at the time, just 50 miles from Canada. I used to take trips over the Ambassador Bridge to Windsor, Ontario, and load up with French-language comic books. Superman in French was such a blast: "*POW! Prend ça; vous mal faiseur!*" ("Pow! Take that; you evildoer!"). Of course, it was necessary to study traditional textbooks to get all the nuance of the language, but the comics helped enormously and my knowledge of French quickly outpaced my German (I couldn't get any German comics).

This is the value of Gehring and Batista's *CrimComics*. In these days of endless television channels, computer games, keg parties, and whatever else young folks get up to, it is difficult to get many students to actually crack a textbook. Gehring and Batista's well-crafted *CrimComics* tell the same story as many texts, even if traditionalists wince at the notion. Of course, as a writer of textbooks myself, I realize that when information is presented in this format, the fine nuances have to be ignored and the qualifiers must be edited out, but this is compensated for when one realizes that this format is more likely to engage these kind of students than a dense text. The information contained in *CrimComics* is both accurate and well written in student-friendly "chatty" style by authors finely attuned to the biosocial perspective, and contains all the relevant details. It follows in the same tradition as *The Cartoon Guide to Genetics, Marx for Beginners, The Cartoon Guide to Physics*, and *A Very Bloody History of the British (Without the Boring Bits!)*. I have all these books in my library, and I'm not ashamed to say that I learned a lot from these cartoon-festooned books.

Let me conclude with a rousing endorsement of *CrimComics*. Krista Gehring and Michael Batista have done biosocial criminology a big favor by introducing the modern student—too often reluctant to read—to the difficulties inherent in the biosocial perspective. I believe that their approach is one that will be appreciated by today's "visual" students and by professors anxious to get their hands on anything that will help their students to learn.

ANTHONY WALSH
Boise State University

PREFACE

Teaching criminology from a biological perspective can be challenging. Oftentimes, many instructors either give very little attention to or even ignore biological theories when they develop their criminology courses. In addition to this, some textbooks include dated discussions that do not add to the students' knowledge base and understanding as to how biology interacts with environment to influence behavior. My experience, however, is that students are fascinated with this topic. They find the historical theories amusing and bewildering and the current biosocial approaches mind-blowing. It is for this very reason that I believe this issue is an important one, as not only is it important to know history so that it doesn't repeat itself, but we should also show students how it *isn't* repeating itself.

When Mike and I were navigating through our master's degrees at Northeastern University, we both took a class with Nicole (Nicky) Rafter. The course focused on early biological theories of crime, and our text was her book, *Creating Born Criminals*. My final presentation outlined how I used stigmata from Lombroso's criminal anthropology to examine and characterize the villains in the *JLA* (1996) comic book series. Fortunately for me, Nicky took an interest in me, and trusted me to do things above and beyond what students normally do. She had several opportunities to travel internationally and asked me to house-sit her flat in Brookline, MA. On several occasions, Mike would visit me while I house-sat, and we would work out various comic book storylines and draw

thumbnail sketches on the floor of the back porch of Nicky's home. It is remarkable how now, far away from Nicky's back porch, Mike and I are still collaborating, and we have produced this issue that is based on her life's work.

While I learned a great deal about the early biological theories of crime when I pursued my master's degree, I was later exposed to modern biosocial approaches when I obtained my doctoral degree. I was required to take Life-Course Criminology, taught by John Wright, and was immersed in material I had never read before in my other criminology courses. I found the information to be extremely interesting and relevant, so much so that I currently use a criminology textbook for my undergraduate courses that is written by a well-known biosocial criminologist, Anthony Walsh. I use it because it gets the biosocial perspective "right." Now, I am not a biosocial criminologist by any stretch of the imagination, but I see the value in teaching students this material. If we only require students to read and learn material that aligns with our own beliefs about crime, we may be depriving them of learning material that may inspire some deep-seated passion within them.

As with any book project, *CrimComics* consumed much time and effort, perhaps more so than a traditional textbook. Thinking about theory—and, in particular, trying to design a work that best conveys the theories in a visual medium—is fun. Still, with busy lives, finding the space in one's day to carefully research, write, illustrate, ink, and letter the pages of this work is a source of some stress. We were fortunate, however, to have had an amazing amount of support during these times from family, friends, and Oxford University Press. We also want to acknowledge the talents of Pat Pollard and Cheryl Wallace. Pat's talent generated the inks for this issue that provided the unique look of the artwork. Cheryl's flair for lettering allowed us to get our ideas across to the readers.

The support of these and so many other individuals has made creating *CrimComics* possible and a rewarding experience for us. We would like to thank the following reviewers: Raymond E. Barranco, Mississippi University; Rose Johnson Bigler, Curry College; Thomas J. Chuda, Bunker Hill Community College; Ellen G. Cohn, Florida International University; Barbara A. Crowson, Norwich University; Anna Divita, University of North Carolina, Charlotte; Dorian Dreyfuss, California State University, East Bay; Kevin R. Duffy, Daytona State College; Paul Kaplan, San Diego State University; Jamie Newsome, University of Texas at San Antonio; Allison Payne, Villanova University; Brenda Riley, Tarleton State University; Anne Strouth, North Central State College; Maria Tcherni-Buzzeo, University of New Haven; Jamie C. Vaske, Western Carolina University; Harold A. Wells, Tennessee State University & Texas Southern Universities. We hope that this and other issues of *CrimComics* will inspire in your students a passion to learn criminological theory.

PART I

Early Biological Theories of Crime

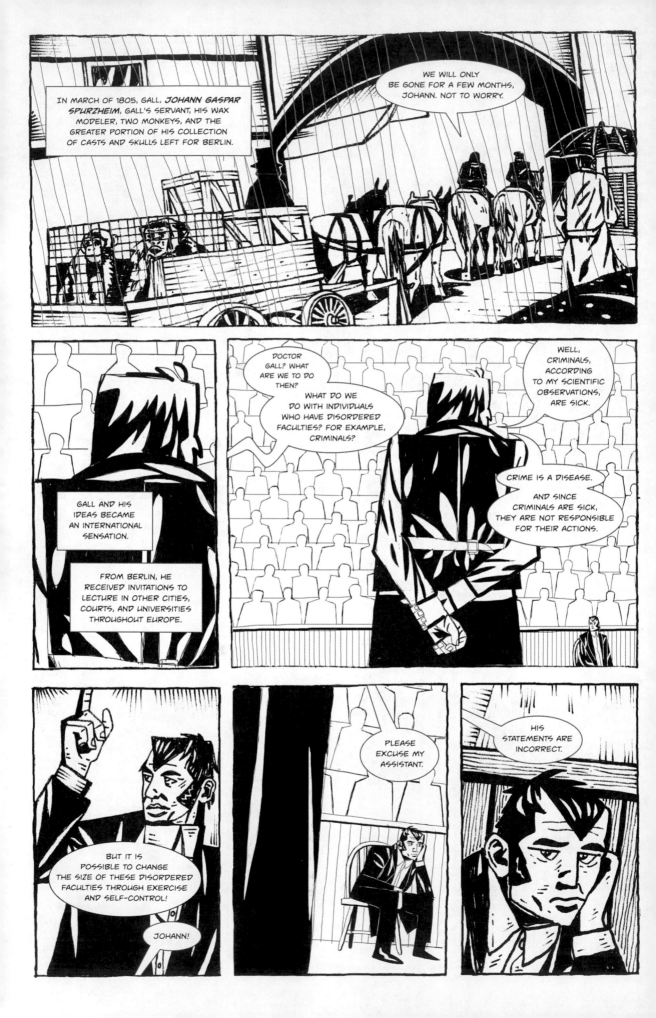

FRANZ JOSEPH GALL'S IDEAS WERE VERY INFLUENTIAL IN CONTRIBUTING TO 19TH-CENTURY THINKING ABOUT CRIMINALITY AS MENTAL ILLNESS.

HE WAS THE FIRST TO CREATE A THEORY OF LOCALIZED MENTAL ILLNESS.

TO HIM, MENTAL ILLNESS WAS BRAIN ILLNESS. BECAUSE OF THIS, HE SPOKE FOR MORE GENTLE HANDLING OF THE MENTALLY ILL.

TODAY, HIS IDEAS ARE VIEWED AS AN IMPORTANT HISTORICAL CONTRIBUTION TO THE CURRENT FIELD OF NEUROPSYCHOLOGY.

JOHANN GASPAR SPURZHEIM'S IDEAS THAT CRIMINALS COULD CHANGE THEIR FACULTIES THROUGH SELF-IMPROVEMENT INFLUENCED IDEAS ABOUT CRIMINAL BEHAVIOR, PUNISHMENT, AND REFORMATION.

THESE IDEAS INSPIRED 19TH-CENTURY CAMPAIGNS AGAINST CAPITAL PUNISHMENT AND IN FAVOR OF BUILDING INSTITUTIONS IN WHICH INMATES COULD STRENGTHEN THEIR NON-CRIMINOGENIC FACULTIES.

PRISONER WILLIAMS? YOU HAVE DEMONSTRATED YOU ARE A CHANGED MAN.

WE ARE MAKING ARRANGEMENTS FOR YOUR RELEASE.

IDEAS CAUSE REACTIONS.

GALAPAGOS ISLANDS, 1831.

THE POPULARITY OF PHRENOLOGY REFLECTED THE PUBLIC'S GROWING FASCINATION WITH SCIENCE.

THIS FASCINATION WOULD BE STRENGTHENED WITH THE PUBLICATIONS OF AN INFLUENTIAL THEORIST WHOSE IDEAS WOULD PAVE THE WAY FOR CONSIDERATION OF TINKERING WITH THE EVOLUTIONARY PROCESS THROUGH SELECTIVE BREEDING.

CHARLES DARWIN MADE A VOYAGE TO THE GALAPAGOS ISLANDS THAT WOULD INFLUENCE HIS THEORY OF EVOLUTION TWENTY YEARS LATER.

IN 1859 HE WROTE *ON THE ORIGIN OF THE SPECIES*, IN WHICH HE ARGUED THAT EVOLUTION OCCURS THROUGH A PROCESS OF NATURAL SELECTION.

TWELVE YEARS LATER, HE WROTE *THE DESCENT OF MAN* (1871) IN WHICH HE SPECIFICALLY PRESENTED THE IDEA ABOUT THE EVOLUTION OF MANKIND.

IN THIS WORK, HE EQUATED DEVELOPMENTAL CHANGE WITH PROGRESS, AND PROPOSED THAT CERTAIN CHARACTERISTICS, SUCH AS THE DESIRE TO LIE OR STEAL, CAN BECOME HEREDITARY.

THIS EMERGING THEORY HAD A DRAMATIC IMPACT ON HOW MANY SCHOLARS VIEWED CRIMINAL BEHAVIOR.

SOME BEGAN TO ASSERT THAT CRIMINALITY COULD BE INHERITED.

THIS LINE OF THINKING, AS WELL AS EMERGING SENTIMENTS THAT CRIMINAL BEHAVIOR COULD BE INHERITED, LED TO THE NEXT STAGE IN THE DEVELOPMENT OF BIOLOGICAL THEORIES OF CRIME: *DEGENERATION THEORY.*

ALARMING, YES, BUT DUGDALE TALKED ABOUT BOTH HEREDITY AND ENVIRONMENT, AND HE THOUGHT THE FAMILY'S POOR ENVIRONMENT WAS TO BLAME FOR THEIR BAD BEHAVIOR.

THEIR ENVIRONMENT PRODUCED THESE HABITS THAT COULD HAVE BECOME HEREDITARY.

BECAUSE OF THIS, HE IS AN ADVOCATE FOR PENAL REFORM, IMPROVED PUBLIC HEALTH, EARLY CHILDHOOD CARE...SOCIAL WELFARE PROGRAMS REALLY.

BUT THOSE THINGS COST MONEY, EDGAR, AND I HAVE HEARD OF OTHER SCHOLARS WHO PROPOSE CRIMINALITY IS INHERITED BUT OFFER A MUCH BETTER SOLUTION IN MY MIND...

CLARENCE, I'M SURE YOU ARE DYING TO TELL ME OF THESE IDEAS, BUT I GROW WEARY OF THIS TALK.

YOU CERTAINLY KNOW HOW TO TURN A MOOD TO MORBID.

REALLY, EDGAR! ALL I'M TRYING TO DO IS EDUCATE YOU! DON'T YOU WANT TO HEAR OF THE ITALIAN PHYSICIAN CESARE LOMBROSO?

HE WROTE A FASCINATING WORK PUBLISHED A YEAR BEFORE DUGDALE PUBLISHED HIS JUKES STUDY.

OR SHALL I SPEAK OF *EUGENICS*?

NO.

THESE NOTIONS REGARDING IDENTIFYING PEOPLE WHO WERE "LESSER STOCK" CAME AT A TIME WHEN THERE WAS TREMENDOUS GROWTH IN AMERICAN CITIES DUE TO URBANIZATION AND IMMIGRATION.

WITH THE INFLUX OF PEOPLE INTO URBAN CENTERS, MANY WERE ALARMED BY ALL OF THE DIFFERENT TYPES OF PEOPLE THEY WERE NOW ENCOUNTERING IN THE CITIES.

CRIME RATES WENT UP, AND MANY STRUGGLED TO PROVIDE EXPLANATIONS FOR THE INCREASE IN CRIMINAL ACTIVITY.

SOME BELIEVED THAT CERTAIN INDIVIDUALS AND ETHNIC GROUPS WERE INFERIOR TO OTHERS AND THEREFORE DANGEROUS.

INCREASED NUMBERS OF THESE INDIVIDUALS MADE THOSE IN POWER WHO WANTED TO MAINTAIN THE STATUS QUO VERY NERVOUS.

WOMEN WERE ALSO GAINING MORE POWER IN THE UNITED STATES IN THE LATE 19TH CENTURY.

MIDDLE-CLASS WOMEN ENTERED THE PUBLIC SPHERE TO ADVOCATE FOR REFORMS IN THE TREATMENT OF MARGINALIZED GROUPS SUCH AS OTHER WOMEN, CHILDREN, AND THE FEEBLEMINDED.

LIBERTY OR DEATH

VOTES

LIBERTY OR DEATH

FREEDOM FOR WOMEN IS NOT A CRIME

AT THE SAME TIME, WORKING-CLASS WOMEN MOVED INTO THE PAID LABOR FORCE AND STARTED TO BECOME SOCIALLY INDEPENDENT.

THESE CHANGES SET OFF A PUNITIVE REACTION TO FEMALE INDEPENDENCE AND SEXUALITY.

THERE WAS A CALL FOR THE PROTECTION OF SOCIETY AGAINST FEEBLEMINDED WOMEN. THIS OCCURRED BECAUSE PEOPLE BELIEVED WOMEN WERE MORE RESPONSIBLE THAN MEN FOR THE BIRTH AND REARING OF CHILDREN.

MANY REQUESTED STATE CONTROL OVER THESE WOMEN ON THE BASIS THAT THEIR BODIES AND WHAT THEY COULD PRODUCE (THAT IS, BABIES) WERE DANGEROUS TO THE MORAL AND SOCIAL FABRIC OF SOCIETY.

THEREFORE, IT BECAME VERY IMPORTANT TO DEVISE A METHOD TO IDENTIFY THESE FEEBLEMINDED INDIVIDUALS SO AMERICANS COULD BE PROTECTED FROM THEIR ILLICIT EXPLOITS AS WELL AS PREVENT THE REPRODUCTION OF THEIR CRIMINAL OFFSPRING.

GODDARD'S BEST KNOWN WORK, THE KALLIKAK FAMILY,* WAS PUBLISHED IN 1912. THIS WORK SEEMINGLY "PROVED" THE CRIMINALITY OF THE FEEBLEMINDED. THE STORY TRACES TWO BRANCHES OF ONE FAMILY, BOTH SIRED BY MARTIN KALLIKAK, SR. THE FIRST BRANCH BEGAN WITH MARTIN'S ENCOUNTER WITH "A FEEBLE-MINDED GIRL" IN A TAVERN DURING THE REVOLUTIONARY WAR. THIS CHANCE MEETING PRODUCED OVER 480 ILLEGITIMATE, ALCOHOLIC, EPILEPTIC, FEEBLEMINDED, AND CRIMINAL DESCENDANTS. LATER, MARTIN MARRIED "A RESPECTABLE GIRL OF GOOD FAMILY." THEIR 496 DESCENDANTS WERE ALL NORMAL WITH SUPERIOR INTELLIGENCE. THIS STUDY WAS "PROOF" THAT THE FEEBLEMINDED WERE INCLINED TO CRIMINAL BEHAVIOR.
*KALÓS IN GREEK MEANS "GOOD." KAKÓS IN GREEK MEANS "BAD."

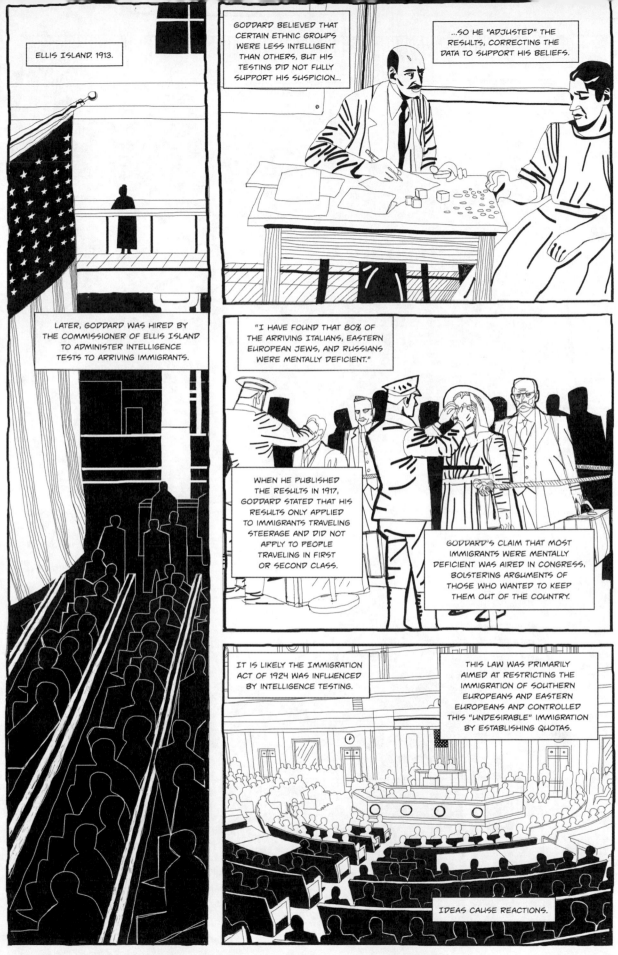

ELLIS ISLAND. 1913.

GODDARD BELIEVED THAT CERTAIN ETHNIC GROUPS WERE LESS INTELLIGENT THAN OTHERS, BUT HIS TESTING DID NOT FULLY SUPPORT HIS SUSPICION...

...SO HE "ADJUSTED" THE RESULTS, CORRECTING THE DATA TO SUPPORT HIS BELIEFS.

LATER, GODDARD WAS HIRED BY THE COMMISSIONER OF ELLIS ISLAND TO ADMINISTER INTELLIGENCE TESTS TO ARRIVING IMMIGRANTS.

"I HAVE FOUND THAT 80% OF THE ARRIVING ITALIANS, EASTERN EUROPEAN JEWS, AND RUSSIANS WERE MENTALLY DEFICIENT."

WHEN HE PUBLISHED THE RESULTS IN 1917, GODDARD STATED THAT HIS RESULTS ONLY APPLIED TO IMMIGRANTS TRAVELING STEERAGE AND DID NOT APPLY TO PEOPLE TRAVELING IN FIRST OR SECOND CLASS.

GODDARD'S CLAIM THAT MOST IMMIGRANTS WERE MENTALLY DEFICIENT WAS AIRED IN CONGRESS, BOLSTERING ARGUMENTS OF THOSE WHO WANTED TO KEEP THEM OUT OF THE COUNTRY.

IT IS LIKELY THE IMMIGRATION ACT OF 1924 WAS INFLUENCED BY INTELLIGENCE TESTING.

THIS LAW WAS PRIMARILY AIMED AT RESTRICTING THE IMMIGRATION OF SOUTHERN EUROPEANS AND EASTERN EUROPEANS AND CONTROLLED THIS "UNDESIRABLE" IMMIGRATION BY ESTABLISHING QUOTAS.

IDEAS CAUSE REACTIONS.

BY THE 1920S, GODDARD BEGAN TO CANDIDLY ADMIT THAT HIS EARLY RESEARCH WAS FLAWED AND THAT THE KALLIKAK FAMILY WAS OUT-OF-DATE.

Kallikaks = obsolete

IT IS LIKELY GODDARD WAS MORE INTERESTED IN PROMOTING EUGENICS THAN CONDUCTING SCIENTIFIC STUDIES.

REGARDLESS, THIS THEORY REGARDING FEEBLEMINDEDNESS CONTRIBUTED TO THE RAPID EXPANSION OF TRAINING SCHOOLS FOR THE FEEBLEMINDED...

...AND THEIR SUBSEQUENT TRANSFORMATION INTO CUSTODIAL INSTITUTIONS WHERE THE DEVELOPMENTALLY DISABLED COULD BE HELD FOR LIFE.

The New
for the Edu
of Feeble-m

UNFORTUNATELY, THESE AMERICAN IDEAS INFLUENCED NAZI GERMANY'S MISSION TO STERILIZE AND EXTERMINATE MILLIONS OF "UNDESIRABLE CITIZENS" DURING THE HOLOCAUST THROUGHOUT WORLD WAR II.

IT WAS FOR THIS VERY REASON THAT THESE THEORIES FELL OUT OF FAVOR IN THE UNITED STATES...

BY THE 1920S AND 1930S, BIOLOGICAL THEORIES WERE REPLACED WITH SOCIOLOGICAL EXPLANATIONS OF CRIME. HOWEVER, THESE BIOLOGICAL THEORIES WERE VALUABLE IN THAT THEY PROMOTED SCIENTIFIC INQUIRY REGARDING CRIMINALS AND CRIMINAL BEHAVIOR. THESE THEORIES ALSO PROVIDE A HISTORICAL FOUNDATION UPON WHICH CURRENT BIOSOCIAL APPROACHES ARE BUILT.

THIS ISSUE BEGAN WITH A DISCUSSION OF PHRENOLOGY, THE FIRST SYSTEMATIC, SCIENTIFIC STUDY OF BEHAVIOR. IT PROPOSED THAT FACULTIES OF THE BRAIN COULD BE FELT IN THE BUMPS AND CONTOURS OF THE SKULL. THE TWO MAJOR PROPONENTS OF THIS THEORY WERE FRANZ JOSEPH GALL AND JOHANN GASPAR SPURZHEIM. THE POPULARITY OF PHRENOLOGY REFLECTED THE PUBLIC'S GROWING FASCINATION WITH SCIENCE. WITH THE ADVENT OF DARWIN'S THEORY OF EVOLUTION, THIS USHERED IN OTHER WAYS OF THEORIZING ABOUT CRIMINAL BEHAVIOR. PROPONENTS OF DEGENERATION THEORY BELIEVED PEOPLE COULD DEVOLVE OVER THE COURSE OF A LIFE SPAN IF THEY ENGAGED IN EXCESSIVE LIVING. THIS WEAKENED PHYSICAL CONDITION WOULD WEAKEN THEIR MORAL CAPACITY AND THUS LEAD THEM TO CRIMINAL BEHAVIOR. THIS EXCESSIVE LIVING WOULD DAMAGE THEM SO MUCH THAT THEY WOULD PASS THIS ON TO THEIR OFFSPRING. THIS WAS EVIDENT IN RICHARD DUGDALE'S WORK *THE JUKES*. HOWEVER, THE MOST NOTABLE CRIMINOLOGIST WHO WAS INFLUENCED BY NOTIONS OF HERITABLE TRAITS WAS CESARE LOMBROSO, ALSO KNOWN AS THE FATHER OF CRIMINOLOGY. HE PROPOSED THAT CRIMINALS WERE EVOLUTIONARILY INFERIOR TO NON-CRIMINALS AND THIS WAS EVIDENCED BY CERTAIN PHYSICAL CHARACTERISTICS. HIS IDEAS SUPPORTED THE NOTION THAT CRIMINALS WERE BORN, NOT MADE. AS TIME WENT ON, HOWEVER, MANY SCHOLARS REALIZED THAT MOST CRIMINALS DID NOT POSSESS THE STIGMATA LOMBROSO SAID THEY DID, SO OTHER WAYS OF IDENTIFYING CRIMINALS BECAME NECESSARY. HENRY GODDARD TRANSLATED ALFRED BINET'S INTELLIGENCE TEST INTO ENGLISH AND USED THIS TO IDENTIFY FEEBLEMINDED INDIVIDUALS. FEEBLEMINDED INDIVIDUALS WERE DEVELOPMENTALLY DISABLED PERSONS WHO WERE ALSO BELIEVED TO BE INNATELY CRIMINAL AND WHO COULD PASS ON THEIR CRIMINALITY TO FUTURE GENERATIONS THROUGH REPRODUCTION. ALTHOUGH GODDARD LATER ADMITTED THAT HIS RESEARCH WAS FLAWED, MANY POLICIES WERE ENACTED TO KEEP FEEBLEMINDED INDIVIDUALS SEPARATE FROM THE REST OF SOCIETY AND TO REMOVE THEIR ABILITY TO REPRODUCE.

BY THE 1920S AND 1930S, THESE THEORIES FELL OUT OF FAVOR AND WERE REPLACED WITH SOCIOLOGICAL EXPLANATIONS OF CRIME.

Key Terms

Franz Joseph Gall
Phrenology
Johann Gaspar Spurzheim
Charles Darwin
Degeneration Theory
Richard Dugdale
Eugenics
Cesare Lombroso
Criminal Anthropology
Atavisms
Feebleminded
Henry Goddard
Buck v. Bell (1927)
Stigmata

Discussion Questions

What is an atavism? What evidence did Lombroso propose supported the existence of atavisms?

What is eugenics?

What were some criticisms of early biological theories of crime?

Suggested Readings

Darwin, C. (1859/2003). *The origin of the species*. New York: Signet Publishing.
Darwin, C. (1871/2004). *The descent of man*. London: Penguin Classics.
Dugdale, R. (1910/2008). *The Jukes*. Whitefish, MT: Kessinger Publishing.
Goddard, H. (2008). *The Kallikak family: A study in the heredity of feeble-mindedness*. CreateSpace Independent Publishing Platform.
Lombroso, C. (1876/2006). *Criminal man*. Durham, NC: Duke University Press.
Lombroso, C. (2010). *The female offender*. Charleston, SC: Nabu Press.
Rafter, N. (1997). *Creating born criminals*. Urbana: University of Illinois Press.
Rafter, N. (2008). *The criminal brain: Understanding biological theories of crime*. New York: NYU Press.
Rafter, N. (2009). *The origins of criminology: A reader*. Abingdon, UK: Routledge-Cavendish.

PART 2

Biosocial Approaches

"BIOLOGICAL EXPLANATIONS OF CRIMINAL BEHAVIOR WERE POPULAR IN THE UNITED STATES UNTIL APPROXIMATELY THE 1930S. THEIR DECLINE COINCIDED WITH MANY FACTORS THAT EMERGED AT THIS TIME. THESE INCLUDED WORLD WAR II AND NAZI GERMANY'S USE OF EXTERMINATION CAMPS TO ELIMINATE 'BIOLOGICALLY INFERIOR PEOPLE.' THE VERY THINGS THAT ARE UPSETTING YOU NOW, RAQUEL. BUT CITIES WERE GROWING EXPONENTIALLY DURING THIS TIME PERIOD DUE TO THE INDUSTRIAL REVOLUTION AND HUGE WAVES OF INDIVIDUALS MOVING FROM THE SOUTH TO NORTHERN URBAN AREAS. ALSO, A HUGE INFLUX OF INDIVIDUALS WERE IMMIGRATING TO THE UNITED STATES FROM OTHER COUNTRIES WITH THE HOPE OF A BETTER LIFE. CRIME IN URBAN AREAS SKYROCKETED. BECAUSE OF THIS, SOCIOLOGICAL EXPLANATIONS OF CRIME EMERGED AND GAINED POPULARITY."

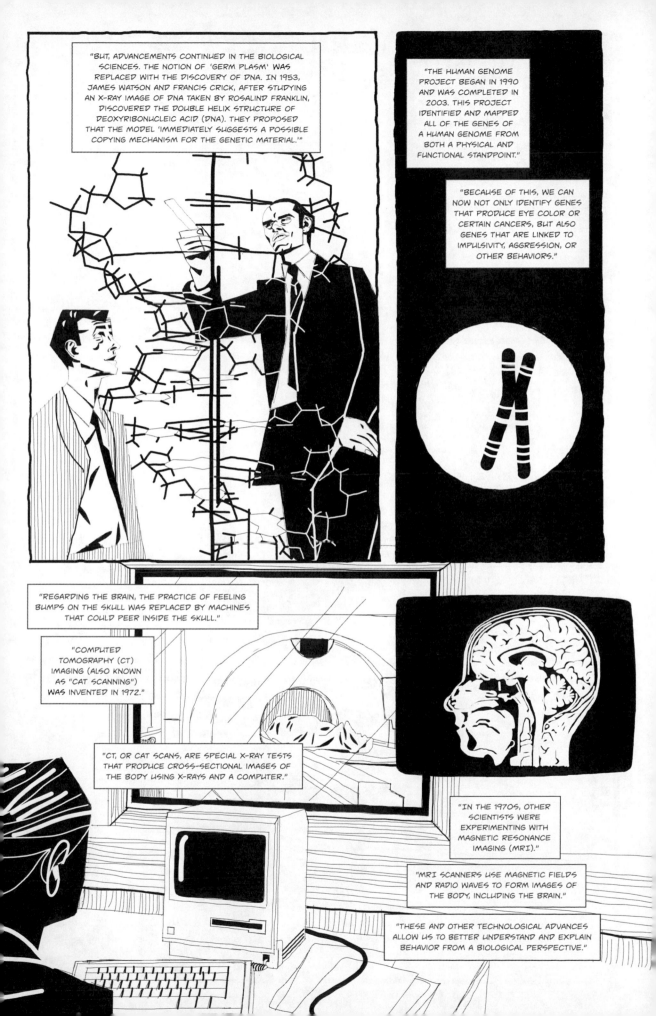

"BUT, ADVANCEMENTS CONTINUED IN THE BIOLOGICAL SCIENCES. THE NOTION OF 'GERM PLASM' WAS REPLACED WITH THE DISCOVERY OF DNA. IN 1953, JAMES WATSON AND FRANCIS CRICK, AFTER STUDYING AN X-RAY IMAGE OF DNA TAKEN BY ROSALIND FRANKLIN, DISCOVERED THE DOUBLE HELIX STRUCTURE OF DEOXYRIBONUCLEIC ACID (DNA). THEY PROPOSED THAT THE MODEL 'IMMEDIATELY SUGGESTS A POSSIBLE COPYING MECHANISM FOR THE GENETIC MATERIAL.'"

"THE HUMAN GENOME PROJECT BEGAN IN 1990 AND WAS COMPLETED IN 2003. THIS PROJECT IDENTIFIED AND MAPPED ALL OF THE GENES OF A HUMAN GENOME FROM BOTH A PHYSICAL AND FUNCTIONAL STANDPOINT."

"BECAUSE OF THIS, WE CAN NOW NOT ONLY IDENTIFY GENES THAT PRODUCE EYE COLOR OR CERTAIN CANCERS, BUT ALSO GENES THAT ARE LINKED TO IMPULSIVITY, AGGRESSION, OR OTHER BEHAVIORS."

"REGARDING THE BRAIN, THE PRACTICE OF FEELING BUMPS ON THE SKULL WAS REPLACED BY MACHINES THAT COULD PEER INSIDE THE SKULL."

"COMPUTED TOMOGRAPHY (CT) IMAGING (ALSO KNOWN AS "CAT SCANNING") WAS INVENTED IN 1972."

"CT, OR CAT SCANS, ARE SPECIAL X-RAY TESTS THAT PRODUCE CROSS-SECTIONAL IMAGES OF THE BODY USING X-RAYS AND A COMPUTER."

"IN THE 1970S, OTHER SCIENTISTS WERE EXPERIMENTING WITH MAGNETIC RESONANCE IMAGING (MRI)."

"MRI SCANNERS USE MAGNETIC FIELDS AND RADIO WAVES TO FORM IMAGES OF THE BODY, INCLUDING THE BRAIN."

"THESE AND OTHER TECHNOLOGICAL ADVANCES ALLOW US TO BETTER UNDERSTAND AND EXPLAIN BEHAVIOR FROM A BIOLOGICAL PERSPECTIVE."

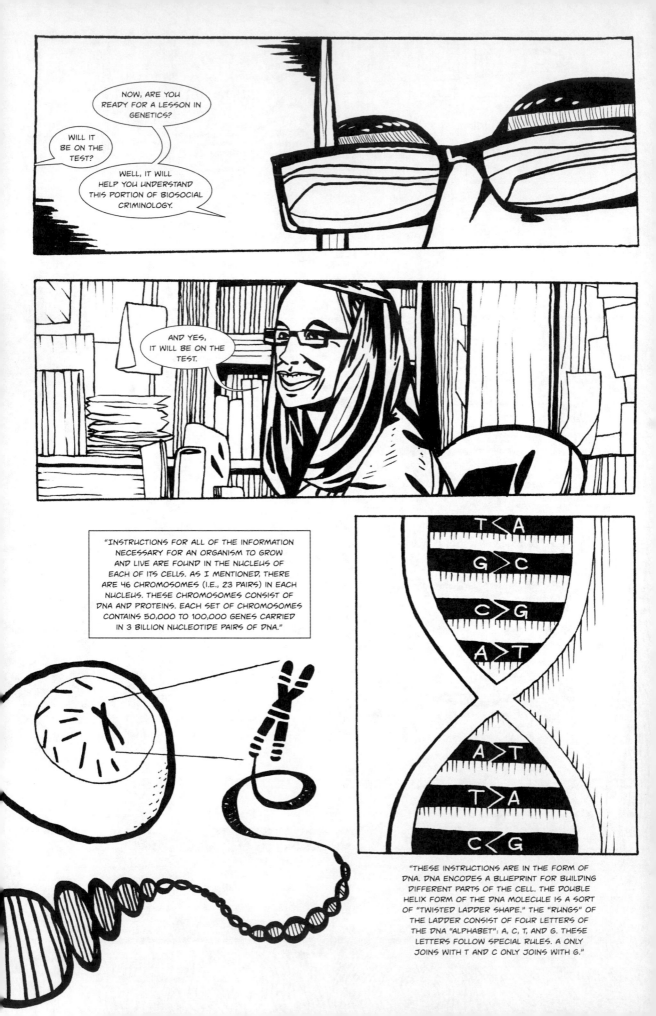

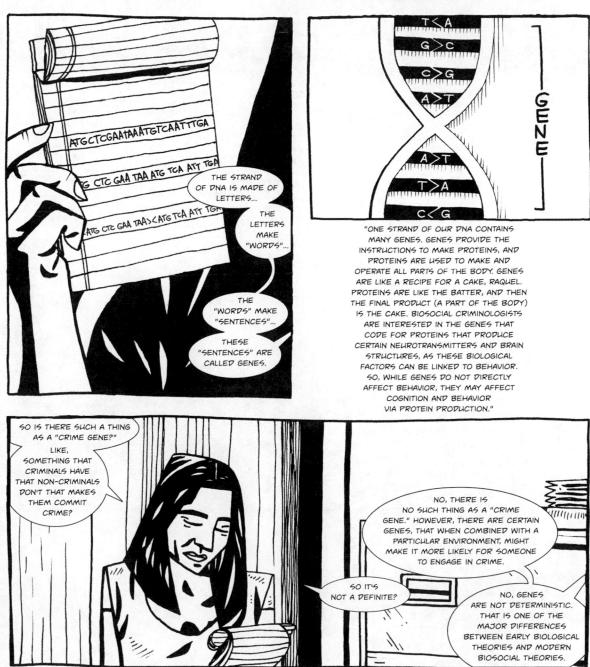

"EVIDENCE FROM TWIN AND ADOPTION STUDIES SUGGESTS THAT BEHAVIORS AND PERSONALITY TRAITS ARE MODERATELY TO HIGHLY HERITABLE. SOME STUDIES COMPARE THE BEHAVIORS OF IDENTICAL TWINS (WHO SHARE 100% OF THEIR DNA) TO THOSE OF FRATERNAL TWINS (WHO SHARE 50% OF THEIR DNA). IF ONE TWIN ENGAGES IN CRIMINAL BEHAVIOR, WE LOOK TO SEE IF THE OTHER TWIN DOES TOO."

"IF GENETICS PLAY A MAJOR ROLE IN DETERMINING THE CRIMINALITY OF INDIVIDUALS, THEN IDENTICAL TWINS WOULD HAVE A SIGNIFICANTLY HIGHER CONCORDANCE RATE (RATE AT WHICH TWIN PAIRS SHARE EITHER A TRAIT OR LACK OF THE TRAIT) FOR OFFENDING THAN FRATERNAL TWINS. OTHER STUDIES LOOK AT IDENTICAL TWINS WHO WERE SEPARATED AT BIRTH. THESE STUDIES FOUND THAT THE TWIN PAIRS OFTEN SHOWED VERY SIMILAR TENDENCIES FOR CRIMINALITY. SOMETIMES MORE THAN THOSE SEEN IN CONCORDANCE RATES FOR IDENTICAL TWINS REARED TOGETHER."

BUT, TO TRY TO FIGURE OUT WHICH IS MOST IMPORTANT, GENES OR ENVIRONMENT, IS PRETTY SILLY.

THEY ALWAYS WORK TOGETHER, SOMETIMES ONE INFLUENCING THE OTHER.

GENE-ENVIRONMENT CORRELATION (RGE) MEANS THAT GENES AND ENVIRONMENTS ARE RELATED.

FOR EXAMPLE, EVOCATIVE RGE REFERS TO THE WAY OTHERS REACT TO YOU BASED ON YOUR BEHAVIOR (WHICH HAS A GENETIC BASIS).

"LET'S ASSUME YOU WERE A PLEASANT BABY AND HAD A GOOD TEMPERAMENT."

"I TOTALLY WAS!"

"HAHA! WELL, THIS WOULD HAVE EVOKED A CERTAIN RESPONSE FROM YOUR PARENTS AND OTHERS IN YOUR ENVIRONMENT AND AFFECTED HOW THEY INTERACTED WITH YOU. IF YOU HAD A SIBLING WHO HAD A DIFFICULT TEMPERAMENT AND TEMPER-TANTRUMED ALL THE TIME, THIS WOULD EVOKE A VERY DIFFERENT RESPONSE FROM YOUR PARENTS AND OTHERS IN HIS OR HER ENVIRONMENT. PASSIVE RGE MEANS YOUR BIOLOGICAL PARENTS PROVIDE YOU WITH GENES LINKED TO CERTAIN TRAITS AND AN ENVIRONMENT FAVORABLE FOR THEIR EXPRESSION. FOR EXAMPLE, YOUR PARENTS ARE INTELLIGENT, SO THEY PASSED ON GENES TO YOU THAT LED TO ABOVE AVERAGE INTELLIGENCE AS WELL AS PROVIDED AN ENVIRONMENT IN WHICH INTELLECTUAL BEHAVIOR WAS MODELED AND REINFORCED."

"MY PARENTS DID BUY ME A LOT OF BOOKS, TOOK ME TO MUSEUMS, AND ENCOURAGED ME TO GET GOOD GRADES..."

"SEE, THEY PROVIDED AN ENVIRONMENT IN WHICH YOUR INTELLIGENCE, WHICH IS HERITABLE, COULD FLOURISH."

44

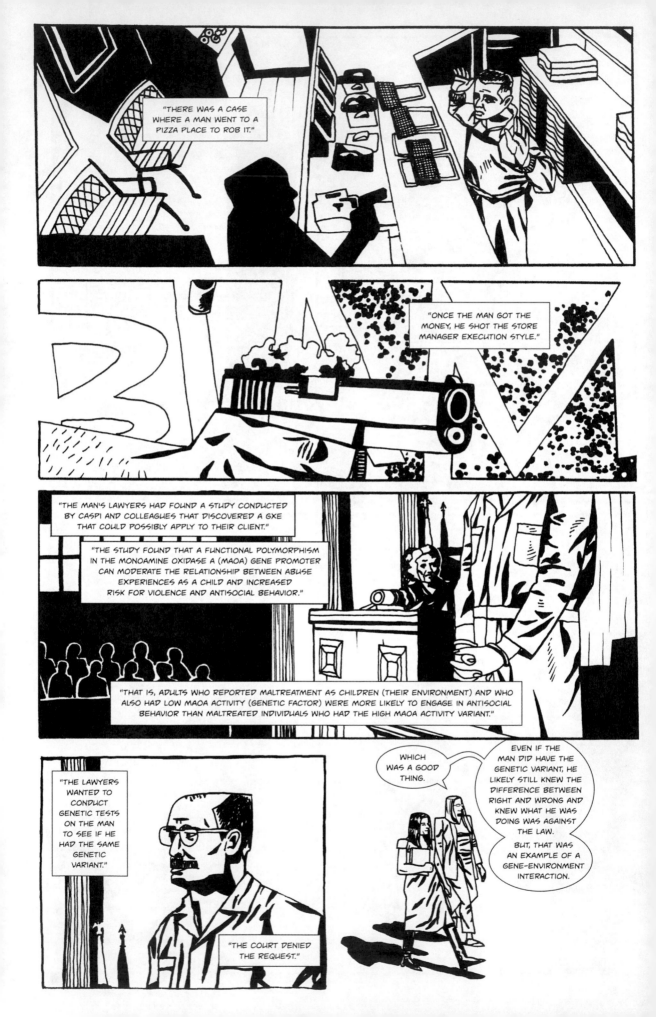

The Synapse

A NEURON IS A NERVE CELL THAT IS THE BASIC BUILDING BLOCK OF THE NERVOUS SYSTEM. THEY ARE SPECIALIZED TO TRANSMIT INFORMATION THROUGHOUT THE BODY. IN ORDER FOR NEURONS TO COMMUNICATE, THEY NEED TO TRANSMIT INFORMATION BOTH WITHIN THE NEURON AND FROM ONE NEURON TO ANOTHER. THIS PROCESS UTILIZES BOTH ELECTRICAL SIGNALS AS WELL AS CHEMICAL MESSENGERS. THE **DENDRITES** OF NEURONS RECEIVE INFORMATION FROM SENSORY RECEPTORS OR OTHER NEURONS. THIS INFORMATION IS THEN PASSED DOWN TO THE **CELL BODY** AND ON TO THE **AXON**. ONCE THE INFORMATION HAS ARRIVED AT THE AXON, IT TRAVELS DOWN THE LENGTH OF THE AXON IN THE FORM OF AN ELECTRICAL SIGNAL KNOWN AS AN **ACTION POTENTIAL**. ONCE AN ELECTRICAL IMPULSE HAS REACHED THE END OF AN AXON, THE INFORMATION MUST BE TRANSMITTED ACROSS THE **SYNAPTIC GAP** TO THE DENDRITES OF THE ADJOINING NEURON. NEUROTRANSMITTERS ARE NEEDED TO SEND THE INFORMATION FROM ONE NEURON TO THE NEXT. NEUROTRANSMITTERS ARE CHEMICAL MESSENGERS THAT ARE RELEASED FROM THE AXON TERMINALS TO CROSS THE SYNAPTIC GAP AND REACH THE RECEPTOR SITES OF OTHER NEURONS. THERE ARE CERTAIN NEUROTRANSMITTERS THAT ARE OF PARTICULAR INTEREST FOR BIOSOCIAL CRIMINOLOGISTS. TOO MUCH OR TOO LITTLE OF THEM IN THE BRAIN CAN AFFECT AN INDIVIDUAL'S BEHAVIOR.

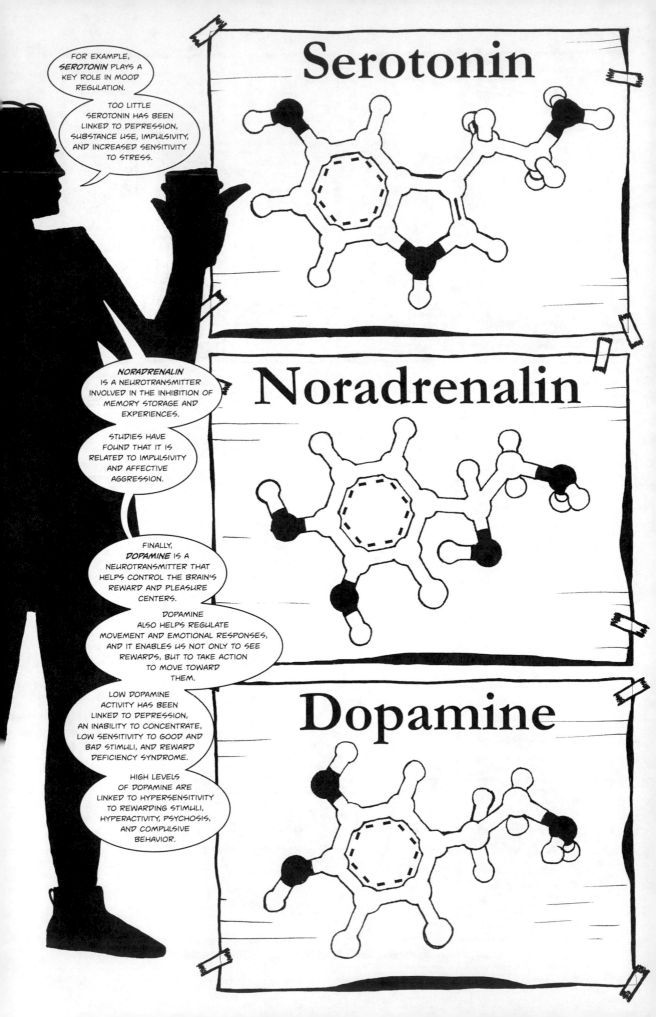

The Human Brain

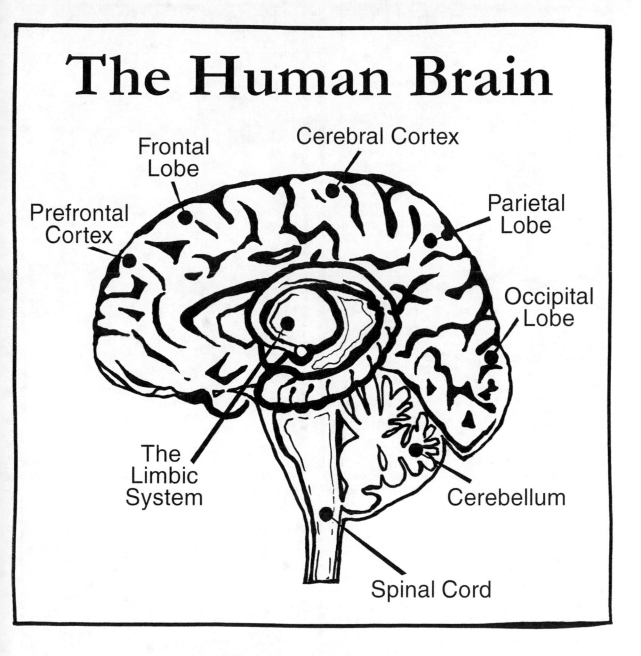

Frontal Lobe

Cerebral Cortex

Parietal Lobe

Prefrontal Cortex

Occipital Lobe

The Limbic System

Cerebellum

Spinal Cord

"WELL, THERE ARE SEVERAL REGIONS OF THE BRAIN THAT BIOSOCIAL CRIMINOLOGISTS ARE VERY INTERESTED IN."

"THE FIRST REGION IS THE **PREFRONTAL CORTEX**. THIS BRAIN REGION CARRIES OUT **EXECUTIVE FUNCTIONS**. EXECUTIVE FUNCTION IS A CONCEPT TO DESCRIBE A LOOSELY DEFINED COLLECTION OF BRAIN PROCESSES WHICH ARE RESPONSIBLE FOR PLANNING, COGNITIVE FLEXIBILITY, ABSTRACT THINKING, RULE ACQUISITION, INITIATING APPROPRIATE ACTIONS AND INHIBITING INAPPROPRIATE ACTIONS, AND SELECTING RELEVANT SENSORY INFORMATION."

"THE SECOND AREA IS THE **LIMBIC SYSTEM**. THIS SYSTEM AND ITS STRUCTURES ARE LOCATED DEEP INSIDE THE BRAIN. THESE STRUCTURES ARE INVOLVED IN MOTIVATION, EMOTION, LEARNING, AND MEMORY. IT IS ALSO CONNECTED WITH THE BRAIN'S PLEASURE CENTER. IT HAS OFTEN BEEN CONSIDERED PART OF OUR 'PRIMITIVE BRAIN,' AS IT CONTROLS BEHAVIORS THAT ARE ESSENTIAL FOR SELF-PRESERVATION, SUCH AS FEEDING, FLEEING, FIGHTING, AND PROCREATION."

BUT NOW THAT YOU UNDERSTAND IT, RAQUEL, HOW COULD WE USE THIS INFORMATION TO PREVENT CRIMINAL BEHAVIOR?

WELL, I THINK EARLY INTERVENTIONS WOULD HELP.

GOOD, RAQUEL-- THINGS LIKE HEAD START OR THE PERRY PRESCHOOL PROJECT.

ALSO, GOOD PRENATAL CARE WOULD ALSO HELP. LIKE MAKING SURE MOTHERS ARE HEALTHY AND NOT DOING ANYTHING THAT MIGHT DAMAGE THE FETUS'S BRAIN IN UTERO.

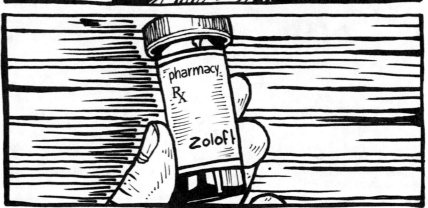

IF PEOPLE HAD TOO LITTLE OR TOO MUCH OF A NEUROTRANSMITTER, THEY COULD TAKE MEDICATION TO BALANCE IT OUT

pharmacy
Rx
Zoloft

AND IF GENES NEED AN ENVIRONMENT TO EXPRESS THEMSELVES, WE CAN CHANGE THE ENVIRONMENT SO THE GENE WON'T GET EXPRESSED OR TURNED ON.

RAQUEL, YOU'RE GOING TO DO JUST FINE ON THE NEXT EXAM.

THIS ISSUE BEGAN WITH A DISCUSSION OF HOW ADVANCEMENTS IN THE BIOLOGICAL SCIENCES LED TO BETTER UNDERSTANDINGS OF BEHAVIOR FROM A BIOLOGICAL PERSPECTIVE. BIOLOGICALLY INFORMED CRIMINOLOGY IS TERMED BIOSOCIAL. "BIO" ACKNOWLEDGES THE BIOLOGY WHILE "SOCIAL" EMPHASIZES ENVIRONMENT. ONE BIOSOCIAL APPROACH IS IN THE AREA OF GENETICS. GENETICS IS THE SCIENTIFIC STUDY OF HEREDITY. GENES PROVIDE THE INSTRUCTIONS TO MAKE PROTEINS, AND PROTEINS ARE USED TO MAKE AND OPERATE ALL PARTS OF THE BODY. GENES INTERACT WITH THE ENVIRONMENT TO AFFECT BEHAVIOR AND PERSONALITY TRAITS. BEHAVIOR GENETICS FOCUSES ON HOW MUCH HEREDITY AND ENVIRONMENT CONTRIBUTE TO BEHAVIOR AND PERSONALITY TRAITS. THIS CAN BE DETERMINED BY LOOKING AT TWIN AND ADOPTION STUDIES. ANOTHER WAY TO DETERMINE HOW GENES AND ENVIRONMENT WORK TOGETHER IS TO EXAMINE GENE-ENVIRONMENT CORRELATIONS. ANOTHER BRANCH OF GENETICS IS MOLECULAR GENETICS. THIS FOCUSES ON GENE-ENVIRONMENT INTERACTIONS AND HOW TWO DIFFERENT GENOTYPES RESPOND TO THE SAME ENVIRONMENT IN DIFFERENT WAYS.

THIS ISSUE ALSO DISCUSSED HOW THE BRAIN CAN BE VERY INFLUENTIAL ON OUR BEHAVIOR. NEUROTRANSMITTERS LIKE SEROTONIN, NORADRENALIN, AND DOPAMINE ARE CHEMICAL MESSENGERS IN THE BRAIN THAT ARE RELEASED SO THE NEURONS CAN COMMUNICATE WITH ONE ANOTHER. TOO MUCH OR TOO LITTLE OF THEM IN THE BRAIN CAN AFFECT AN INDIVIDUAL'S BEHAVIOR. ONE THEORY THAT LINKS NEUROTRANSMITTERS TO BEHAVIOR IS REWARD DOMINANCE THEORY. THIS THEORY POSITS THAT BEHAVIOR IS REGULATED BY TWO OPPOSING MECHANISMS, THE BEHAVIORAL ACTIVATING SYSTEM (BAS) AND THE BEHAVIORAL INHIBITION SYSTEM (BIS). SPECIFIC REGIONS OF THE BRAIN ARE ALSO LINKED TO BEHAVIOR. PREFRONTAL DYSFUNCTION THEORY POSITS THAT THE FRONTAL LOBES OF CRIMINALS ARE NOT FUNCTIONING PROPERLY. IF THERE IS AN ISSUE, THE WAYS WE CAN MINIMIZE THE EFFECT GENES AND THE BRAIN MAY HAVE ON MALADAPTIVE AND CRIMINAL BEHAVIORS CAN BE THROUGH EARLY INTERVENTIONS, PHARMACOLOGICAL TREATMENT, PRENATAL CARE, OR BY CHANGING THE ENVIRONMENT.

Key Terms

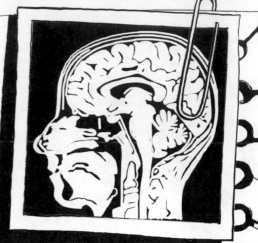

Genes
Chromosomes
DNA
Behavior Genetics
Heritability (h^2)
Twin Studies
Adoption Studies
Gene-Environment Correlation (rGE)
Evocative rGE
Passive rGE
Active rGE
Gene-Environment Interaction (GxE)
Molecular Genetics
Epigenetics
Neurons
Neurotransmitters
Dendrites
Cell Body
Axon
Action Potential
Synaptic Gap
Serotonin
Noradrenalin
Dopamine
Reward Dominance Theory
Behavioral Activating System (BAS)
Behavioral Inhibition System (BIS)
Prefrontal Cortex
Limbic System
Prefrontal Dysfunction Theory

Discussion Questions

Is there any validity to family studies in determining the role of genetics in criminal behavior? Why or why not?

How do the concepts of evocative rGE, passive rGE, and active rGE apply to your own life? Give examples for how each concept appears in your life.

Explain what neurotransmitters are and describe how specific neurotransmitters can influence criminal behavior.

What types of policy implications would you support based on the information provided by this section of the text?

Suggested Readings

Caspi, A., et al. (2002). *Role of genotype in the cycle of violence in maltreated children*. Science, 297(5582), 851-854.
Dalgaard, O. S., & Kringlen, E. (1976). *A Norwegian study of criminality*. British Journal of Criminology, 16, 213-232.
Mednick, S. A., Gabrielli, W., & Hutchings, B. (1984). *Genetic influences in criminal convictions: Evidence from an adoption cohort*. Science, 224, 891-894.
Mednick, S. A., & Volavka, J. (1980). *Biology and crime*. In N. Morris and M. Tonry (Eds.), Crime and justice: An annual review of research (Vol. 2, pp. 85-158). Chicago: University of Chicago Press.
Walsh, A. (2012). *Criminology: The essentials*. Los Angeles: Sage Publications.
Wright, J., Tibbets, S., & Daigle, L. (2008). *Criminals in the making*. Los Angeles: Sage Publications.